# Business Model Innovation Strategy: Achieving Sustainable Growth Through Effective Advertising

# Dedication

*To*

*My little angel*

*Stephnie Chinomnso Irobiko*

# *Table of Contents*

## Chapter 1 .....................................................................................9

1.1 Administrative Summary........................................................9
1.2 Introduction to the Report ...................................................10
1.3 Background of the Study ......................................................12

## Chapter 2 ...................................................................................15

Report on Cadbury...................................................................15
2.1 An Overview of the Company ..............................................15
2.2 Situational Analysis: Current Performance, Productivity and Competitive Position ..............................................................17
2.3 The Meta Model Analysis......................................................22
2.4   Inner Dynamics................................................................27
2.5   The Payoff Concept .........................................................28
2.6   Grammar .........................................................................30
2.7   Cadbury's Major Threat...................................................30
2.8   Solutions from the BSC and SRM ...................................30
2.8.1    The BSC Solution ......................................................30
2.8.2    Solution through the Strategy Map............................32
2.9   Suggestions for Business Transformation.......................34
2.10   Risks of Neglecting the Proposals .................................35
2.11   Consultant's Opinion and Advice ..................................37

## Chapter 3 ...................................................................................39

Evidence Review .....................................................................39
3.0   Introduction to Advertising .............................................39
3.1   The Strategy Road Map Methodology ............................41

| | | |
|---|---|---|
| 3.1.1 | Strategy | 41 |
| 3.2 | Benefits of Strategy Roadmap | 45 |
| 3.3 | Planning with SRM | 46 |
| 3.4 | Implementing and Updating the Strategy Map | 47 |
| 3.5 | SRM Limitations | 47 |
| 3.6 | The Balanced Score Card (BSC) Methodology | 48 |
| 3.7 | BSC as a Management System | 49 |
| 3.8 | Do Companies need a BSC? | 50 |
| 3.9 | Prospective DBA Perspective for Transforming Clients' Business | 51 |

## Chapter 4 .............................................................................53

An Assessment of the Researcher's Employability Enhancement......53

4.1  Personal Qualities Required to Successfully Complete this Assignment..................................................................................53

4.2  Evaluation of the Researcher's Ability for this Academic Task 54

4.3  Related Leadership Skills needed for Personal Development and Career Growth ....................................................................55

References....................................................................................58

# Foreword by the Author

Innovation can only thrive when it emerges from an organization committed to the growth and sustainability of the enterprise. Instead of thinking of cultivating an innovation in isolation, organizations are more successful when they generate a cluster of innovations, manage them side-by-side, and evaluate how they interact as a portfolio of initiatives.

To build a successful business, you need to stop doing random acts of marketing and start following a reliable plan for rapid business growth. Traditionally, creating a marketing plan has been a difficult and time-consuming process, which is why it often doesn't succeed.

Today, advertisers blast consumers with requests or reminders from morning till dawn. Yet advertisements greatly absorb consumers' awareness and have the potential of affecting their thoughts, attitudes, feelings, and decisions.. Advertisement - the heartbeat of marketing in the modern world - is how you persistently forge connections, engage audiences, and establish brand loyalty. It's the key to elevating businesses to new heights.

But can you leverage advertising to the same effect if you're not a multi-national company with a massive budget? The short answer is: "Yes, you can!" You can see rapid growth in your business and build your online presence massively… All you need is a clear understanding of advertising as a strategy roadmap to increasing competitiveness and creating sustainable growth.

*Business Model Innovation Strategy: Achieving Sustainable Growth Through Effective Advertising* explores the immediate and subsequent effects of advertising on consumer choice, sales, and market share. To explain the broad scope of advertising, this publication uses simple terms and ideas in a general sense that encompasses a variety of theories and contexts in which advertising occurs. The book is an asset to students and professionals in various fields, especially those who want to learn more about the application of business analysis tools like SWOT, PESTEL, Strategic Roadmap (SRM), and the Balanced Scorecard (BSC) in real world business settings.

This book will help you:

- Learn the basics of business model innovation, including the latest developments in strategic management and advertising.

- Learn how business model innovation presents new and profitable business opportunities in industries that were considered all but immune to attacks from newcomers.

- Learn how to determine the viability of your current business model.

- Explore new possibilities for value creation by redesigning your firm's business model.

- Receive practical, step-by-step guidance on how to introduce business model innovation in your own company.

- Become well-versed in an important area of business strategy and entrepreneurship.

# Chapter 1

## 1.1 Administrative Summary

Financial globalization, persuasive marketing, and the fast-changing nature of business in international markets have presented consumers with a variety of options regarding goods and services, together with their attendant difficulties in making choices (Adjei et al, 2024; Iqbal Anjum, 2006). Many scholars have therefore delved into identifying what factors influence consumers decision to choose some products or services against similar goods from rival companies (Munir & Bukhari, 2020; Angela Chang & Kukar-Kinney, 2011; Gurley et al, 2005; Cengiz et al, 2024).

Sales promotion in the Nigerian food drink industry is therefore central to innovative business leaders wishing to stay competitive in a global market flooded with assorted goods and services from indigenous and multinational companies. The quest for market shares thus creates a fiercely contested marketplace where benefits from using each product or service must be effectively communicated to consumers through promotional strategies with direct impact on existing or potential customers. The process of achieving competitiveness, on one hand, depends on managers' adaptability to change and innovative strategies and, on the other hand, the quality of value offered to customers and stakeholders (Osanlou & Rezaei, 2024; Zekos, 2003; Baoku et al, 2010; Wills et al, 1990; Akram et al, 2018; McNeill, 2013).

This Consultancy task is presented in three chapters: first, Cadbury's current market position, its productivity level, as well as challenges which are assessed through PESTEL, SWOT, Porter's 5 Forces and the Meta Model; the second part focused on proffering solutions through the Balanced Score Card and Strategy Road Map (SRM), including the benefits and risks of applying the proposed changes. Consequences of failing to adapt to the change and innovative strategies are also outlined together with a review or related literatures. The third part contains the Consultant's reflection on prior experience regarding the module in this report, with highlights.

Findings from this report show that organizations must embrace change and innovation to improve and maximise use of people, process and technology. Organizational mission, values and objectives must also align with strategy and innovation to achieve high-level productivity, profitability and sustainable competitive advantage (Ahlqvist et al, 2010; Binci et al, 2016; Sokolova & Vishnevskiy, 2023).

## 1.2 Introduction to the Report

According to a study conducted by Adeolu and his team of researchers in 2005, advertising is a key factor in strategy and innovation that boosts business performance in the manufacturing sector. The study involving 315 consumers of soft drink who were selected at random in Ile-ife, Ibadan and Lagos,, evaluated the impact of advertising on end users' preference, with focus on

Bournvita, which has been a popular food drink around Nigeria for decades. Results from the empirical study indicate there are discrepancies in the degree of influence among genders, social class and age groups. Out of the 315 survey participants, 38.73% revealed that they chose Bournvita because of the company's appealing ads. 42.62% cited product quality, while 71.43% agreed that captivating advertising is a major marketing tool that companies in every industry should consider for better performance and sustainable growth. This paper therefore examines Cadbury's current situation and how managers and executives can maximise advertising to create competitive advantage, boost sales, and increase profitability across all market segments (Carlos et al, 2018; Baaij & Reinmoeller, 2018).

Branding, according to Michaelidou et al (2021), is a similar strategy to advertising, and must be a top priority for organizations where managers understand its indispensability and invaluable contributions to business growth. Branding does not just describe what companies offer their customers; it serves as a catalyst for building trust, loyalty and support (). Additionally, consumers' perception of a brand is what triggers their decision to buy a product and forgo similar goods from rival companies. However, Gebreselassie and Bougie (2019) argue that branding must provide great value and consumer safety to retain buyers on a long-term basis.

On maximising use of advertising and branding, Michaelidou et al (2021) stated that a company's market position is a function of what marketing strategies are applied or eliminated from the business model. Advertising therefore focuses on winning consumers' loyalty through a consistent delivery of high quality, valuable, and safe goods and services that create positive customer experiences. This highlights the link between marketing/advertising, sales, and long-term survivability of businesses. Advertising also increases customer reach, builds customer awareness of a business/brand, promotes the benefits of using certain products or services, communicates information about a business/brand, increases sales and demand, as well as, fosters long-term relationships between management and customers (Tan et al, 2023; Gebreselassie & Bougie, 2019; Zimand-Sheiner & Earon, 2019; Shi et al, 2022).

Chen (2018) and Lahtinen et al (2020) described advertising as an aspect of the promotional mix which is connected to the 4Ps of marketing—price, product, place and promotion. The researchers also agreed that no company exclusively uses the relationship marketing approach. While managers support use of the traditional marketing concept of 4Ps; the innovative and visionary ones are blending a relationship and transactional marketing mix to achieve more. Research by different scholars indicate the 4Ps of marketing are still dominating relationship concepts and are utilized to some extent. However, firms should use the relationship strategy as a supporting approach (Zineldin & Philipson, 2007; Chen, 2018; Lahtinen et al, 2020).

## 1.3 Background of the Study

According to Kotler (1980), selling concepts have proven that consumers rarely purchase products and/or services from brands with insignificant investments in promotional activities. On this backdrop, the volume of sales documented by Cadbury Nigeria Plc in recent years—despite improvements after disruptions from COVID-19 pandemic—could have been higher if the company had implemented one or more cost-effective promotional strategies (Zhan et al, 2021; Zineldin & Philipson, 2007; Yang et al, 2018; Guedes et al, 2023).

Aggressive marketing strategies, including a mix of public relations, advertising and sales promotion, are some of the strategic road maps through which Cadbury can enhance profitability. However, positive experience gained from using a company's product or service instils loyalty in existing customers and, in turn, attracts more users through service ratings, testimonies, and referrals. According to Chen (2018), social status attached to brands/companies gain more popularity when famous people in the society identify with a company (that is, show public support) or publicize preference for certain products from the brand (Lahtinen et l, 2020; Yang et al, 2018; Guedes et al, 2023).

The success of modern-day print and electronic media advertising shows that the main purpose of advertising isn't only to increase sales volume and revenues by sensitizing people on the existence or benefits of using certain products or services. Advertising further provides entertainment and educates viewers, readers and listeners (Zhan et al, 2021). Zimand-Sheiner and Earon (2019) explained the difference between advertising as science and art, noting that the concept of advertising is better described as a combination of some unique elements selected from social sciences and communication arts (anthropology, drama, psychology etc). Generally, an appealing promotional activity demands possession of quality advertising skills and good use of pictures, jingles, words, colours, slogans, among others, to influence consumer preferences (Huang, 2019; Li et al, 2023).

Notwithstanding the fierce competition against Nestle Nigeria, the subject of this case study, Cadbury Nigeria, has thrived in the food and beverage manufacturing sector since 1956, when it started operations in the West African country. Cadbury first sold imported chocolate products before registering as a public limited company under Cadbury Fry Expert Limited in 1965. Between 1956 and 1969, the company sold a cocoa beverage commonly known as Pronto and a malt beverage, BOURNVITA, which boosted earnings despite the "unappealing" packaging. A solid network of competent wholesale distributors was responsible for such a historical expansion. Cadbury started full-time manufacturing of BOURNIVTA in 1966. However, the recent slide in Cadbury's revenues and overall performance is connected to the stiff competition from local and multinational companies operating in Nigeria's food and beverage drinks industry, particularly Nestle Nigeria Plc, producers of the famous beverage drink, MILO.

This study therefore provides answers to:

1. How has Cadbury performed against market competitors?

2. How can advertising boost competitiveness, profitability and sustainability for manufacturing companies?

# Chapter 2

## REPORT ON CADBURY

### 2.1 AN OVERVIEW OF THE COMPANY

To many Nigerians, Cadbury represents one of most-popular food beverage and confectionary companies. Its headquarters is in Ikeja, Lagos, specifically on Lateef Jakande Road in Agidingbi area of the city from where it competes with a strong rival company, Nestle Nigeria, the famous manufacturer of MILO and Nescafe CERELAC, among other popular products.

Cadbury's product line includes Tom Tom, Eclairs, Buttermint, Malta sweet, Bournvita, Richoco etc. In 1976, the manufacturing giant got listing on the NSE. Quality delivery has since transformed Cadbury into a multinational company. Famous for is corporate social responsibility (CSR) and unique business ideas, Cadbury has impacted on many lives through educational sponsorship, sports, research and development (R&D) and more innovative relationship building strategies. One of its best years before disruptions from the pandemic was 2013 (See Table 1) (Otusanya et al, 2023; Murunga, 2022; Lin et al, 2024).

Cadbury is into production and sale of sugar confectionary, food drinks, and food products although its major business is processing of cocoa for exports, a business it transacts under Stanmark, an affiliated processor where it holds 90% stake and supplies 100% of cocoa demands. **Oyeyimike Adeboye** is the

Managing Director and Executive Director of Cadbury Nigeria Plc. Ogaga Ologe (Finance Director & Director), and Sunil Parthasarathy (Non-Executive Director) are key members of the management team.

*Table 1: How Cadbury Nigeria makes and spends money. Based on latest reported earnings, on an LTM basis.*

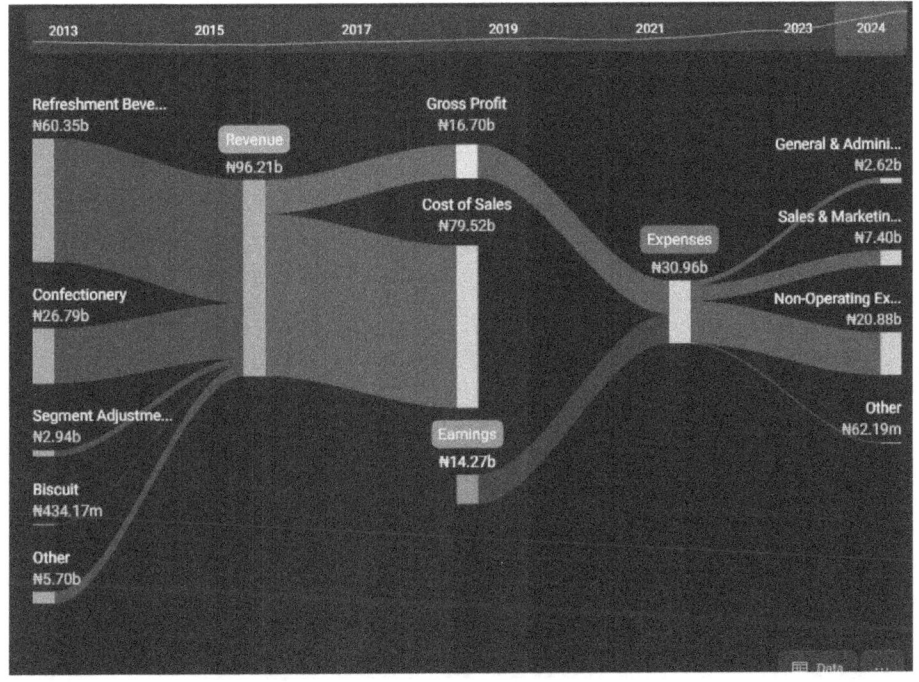

*Source: Simplywall*

Cadbury Schweppes Overseas bought nearly 75% stake in Cadbury Nigeria Plc in 2010 and the remaining 25% is shared between corporate investors and a group of entrepreneurs. The Nigerian food beverage manufacturer started its strategic restructuring process in 2008. However, the change in investment, business process, people and technology—especially in the post

COVID-19 era—have significantly boosted business performance. Positive changes in the current financials also indicate the management must embrace strategy and innovation to strengthen competitiveness. This study thus aims to restore profitability through a methodological approach that also sustains growth by continuously creating value for shareholders and stakeholders.

*Table 2: Cadbury's financial highlights for FY 2022 and FY 2023*

| In thousands of naira | 2023 | 2022 | Change % |
|---|---|---|---|
| Revenue | 80,378,955 | 55,212,617 | 46 |
| Gross profit | 17,337,427 | 7,722,811 | 124 |
| Result from operating activities | 7,872,189 | 194,063 | 3,957 |
| (Loss)/Profit before tax | (28,157,034) | 1,298,410 | (2,269) |
| (Loss)/Profit for the year | (19,089,704) | 583,111 | (3,374) |
| Share capital | 939,101 | 939,101 | - |
| Total equity | (6,513,678) | 13,302,629 | (149) |

*Source: Cadbury Annual Report (31 December 2023)*

## 2.2 SITUATIONAL ANALYSIS: CURRENT PERFORMANCE, PRODUCTIVITY AND COMPETITIVE POSITION

The innovative business approaches applied since 2008 have yielded significant profits despite some fluctuations between 2014 and 2016. For instance, Cadbury's 2011 financial statement showed robust growth in profit, revenue and market share. This remarkable financial performance (See Table 1 and 2) was attributed to debt settlement. In the same year, 2016, profit before tax (PBT) rose by 160% whereas profit after tax (PAT) skyrocketed by 217%. In addition, Cadbury's capital investment has increased since 2010 thereby improving overall performance and cost efficiency and underscoring the short- and long-term benefits of implementing change and innovation strategies—such as advertising—to support value creation.

Cadbury management stated in its 2013 financial statement that plan was in progress to reduce capital investments. The idea was to reduce its share capital ratio to 2:5 and repay about N12bn owed in the company's ordinary share capital and share premium accounts. This financial management decision dashed hopes of Cadbury shareholders expecting about N9.5 profits per share. This sparked huge criticisms from a group of minority shareholders who sought legal solutions against financial losses.

Compensation options from the food beverage manufacturer included keeping the capital for future investment, using it as working capital, or sharing the excess cash to shareholders. A 2013 report from *The Nation* confirmed Cadbury's decision to apply the third option of returning the excess cash to investors based on the need to protect stakeholders' interest and create value through strategic investments. Shareholders protested reasons for Cadbuury's resolution.

For FY11 and FY12, Cadbury documented increase in profit margins. Specifically, Return on Investments (ROI) rose by 29% in 2011 and 19% in 2012, a result the company claimed was below expectations but, in September 2013, announced an 18.2% rise in undocumented ROEs. Its major rival, Nestle, rose by 43% in the same period. Cadbury's average ROE between 2010-13 stood at 7%.

*Image 1: Cadbury's Balance Sheet (FY12 & FY17) with a 3-year financial projection*

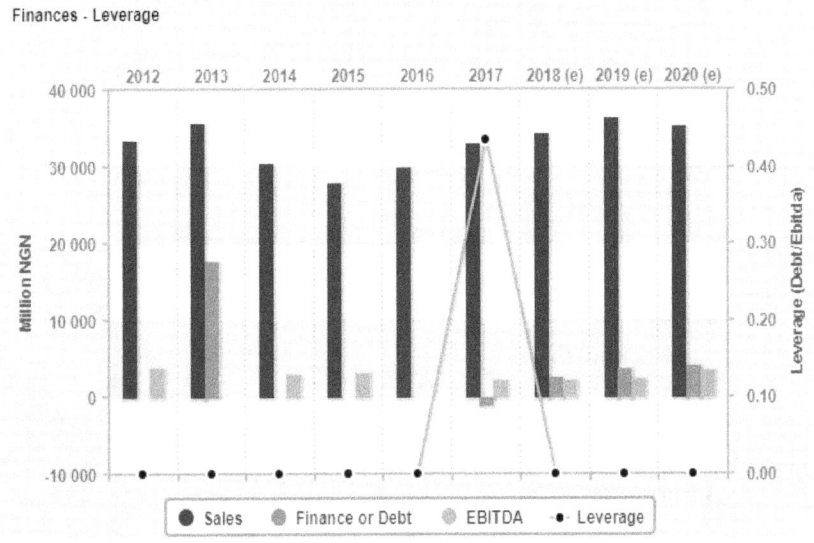

*Source: Cadbury*

Cadbury's financial audit for 2013 indicates that no debt was incurred for FY13. The company documented a cash balance of N16.8bn and an improved working balance totalling N8 bn plus excess cash to pay off all short-term investors. Yet total profits declined by 50% in 2014 (Oludare et al., 2014).

By dint of fluctuations in earnings, Cadbury declared loss of N766.39m in Q2 2017 as confirmed by *Proshare*, a Nigerian financial news website. This downward trend was a follow-up to the huge loss in 2016, when Cadbury lost to its major rival, Nestle, which documented double profits to retain market leadership.

Table 3: Company Financials (Source: The Nigerian Stock Exchange)

| 26th July, 2017: CADBURY PLC | | | |
|---|---|---|---|
| Q2 REPORT FOR THE PERIOD ENDED 30 JUNE | | | |
| | 2017 N'm | 2016 N'm | % Change |
| | JUN | JUN | |
| Revenue | 16,264 | 13,917 | 16.9% |
| Profit before tax | (766.389) | 216.393 | -454.2% |
| Taxation | Nil | (69.246) | #VALUE! |
| Profit after tax | (766.389) | 147.147 | -620.8% |
| Basic Earnings Per Share (kobo) | (41) | 8 | -612.5% |
| Balance Sheet Information | | | |
| Net Assets | 10,530 | 11,057 | -4.8% |
| https://theanalystng.com/nse/ir.php?ref=CADBURY | | | |
| | | | |
| Corporate Declaration | | | |
| Proposed Dividend | Nil | | |
| Proposed Bonus | Nil | | |
| Qualification Date | Nil | | |
| Payment Date | Nil | | |
| Closure Date | Nil | | |
| AGM Date | Nil | | |
| AGM Venue | Nil | | |

Image 2: Company Balance Sheet (Source: Company Annual Report)

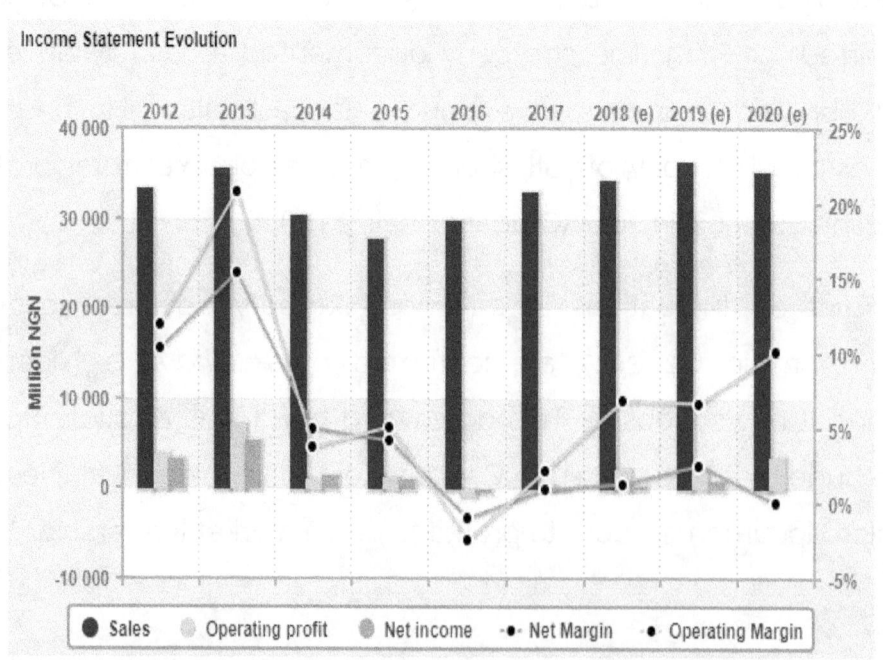

*Image 3: Company Financial Growth Level (Source: Cadbury Annual Report)*

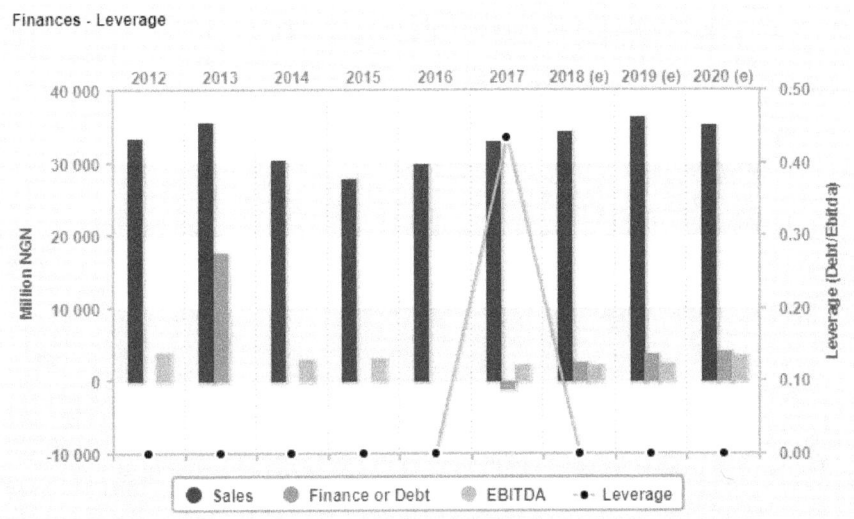

To understand Table 1, 2, and 3 containing financial data of Cadbury Nigeria Plc, readers should view the statistical information as valuation metrics applied by companies or organizations to identify the interrelatedness between value and operational earning capabilities. EBITDA, or earnings before interest, taxes, depreciation, and amortization, is an alternate measure of profitability to net income. By excluding depreciation and amortization as well as taxes and debt payment costs, EBITDA attempts to represent the cash profit generated by the company's operations. In other words, it is a tool applied to understand a company's current business situation, specifically to show whether it is overrated or undervalued (Cormier et al, 2017; Omar Trejo-Pech et al, 2008).

The three tables show that Cadbury has a financial valuation ratio above competitors at an average 13.00, which indicates that its market value is far below competitors in the year(s) under review. The valuation metrics further proves that Cadbury is a low performer among Nigerian manufacturers of beverage food drinks by 9.87.

Table 2: Company Yearly Financial Statement for FY15-FY2017 with a 3-year projection

Annual Income Statement Data

| Fiscal Period December | Actuals in M NGN | | | Estimates in M NGN | | |
|---|---|---|---|---|---|---|
| | 2015 | 2016 | 2017 | 2018 | 2019 | 2020 |
| Sales | 27 825 | 29 979 | 33 079 | 34 363 | 36 487 | 35 282 |
| EBITDA | 3 205 | - | 2 303 | 2 343 | 2 441 | 3 563 |
| Operating profit (EBIT) | 1 421 | -733 | 711 | 2 343 | 2 441 | 3 563 |
| Pre-Tax Profit (EBT) | 1 577 | -563 | 350 | 651 | 1 362 | - |
| Net income | 1 153 | -296 | 300 | 443 | 926 | - |
| P/E ratio | - | - | - | 60,4 | 29,0 | - |
| EPS (NGN) | 0,61 | - | 0,16 | 0,24 | 0,50 | - |
| Dividend per Share (NGN) | 0,65 | 0,65 | - | 0,20 | 0,50 | - |
| Yield | - | - | - | 1,38% | 3,45% | - |
| Reference price (NGN) | | | | 14.5 | 14.5 | 14.5 |
| Announcement Date | 05/31/2016 04:20am | 03/21/2017 01:16pm | 03/19/2018 08:02pm | - | - | - |

Lastly, the manufacturer's financial valuation ratio has been on constant fall for a period of 3 years (2015 – 2018), with minimal improvement expected from 2019. The 3-year financial projection falls below an industry average of 12.2.

## 2.3 THE META MODEL ANALYSIS

In Beinhocker's 2016 work, the researcher explained that the three-fold challenges to organizational growth are: bureaucratic bottlenecks, managerial incompetence due to inflexibility and poor use or under-development of human and material capital. The named factors exert influence on how grammar and inner dynamics adapt to change and innovation strategies, especially where there's pressure from the outer dynamics. This Consultancy study therefore aims at helping Cadbury management improve productivity through innovative business practices and culture shift.

According to the chief proponent, Matthews (2017), a Meta model is a special framework for examining all existing high-impact elements within an organization's business environment. This makes the analytical tool suitable for this study on Cadbury (Russo et al, 2018; Ferber & Gutknecht, 1998).

The analytic framework from Matthews offers a comprehensive understanding of the outer dynamics which he divided into two factors namely: competitive and macro dynamic factors.

Under macro dynamics, the researcher identified governmental policies on production and sourcing or raw materials, CSR, environmental responsibilities, employment law, legal costs, technological development and the capital-intensive nature of multinational corporations. Other factors include investment in ICT, marketing and R&D, as well as the loss from importation of machinery which are required by local manufacturers for increased productivity.

According to Matthews (2017), the Competitive factors, which are also known as co-competitive dynamics, examines multifaceted challenges faced to consumers, investors and stakeholders. In addition, these elements from the external environment determine business performance, particularly in sales, marketing and profit margins. Accordingly, these processes are explained through a PEST Analysis, the analytical model through which the Consultant identifies and presents Cadbury's business opportunities and threats to achieving sustainable competitive advantage. Details appear below in the following images.

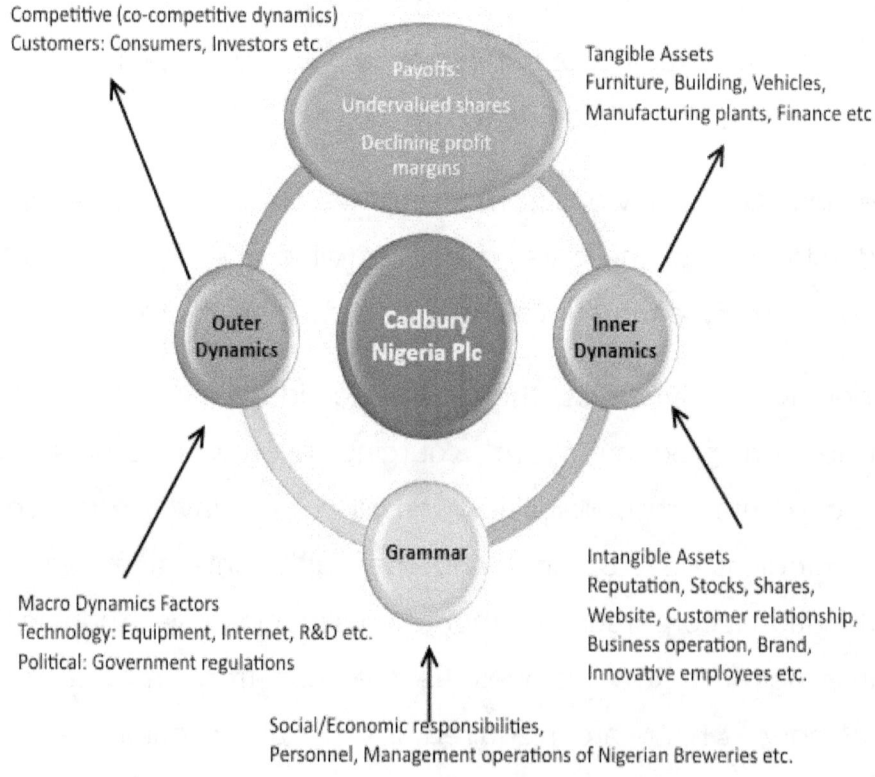

Image 4: The Meta Model Concept by Matthews Robin (2017)

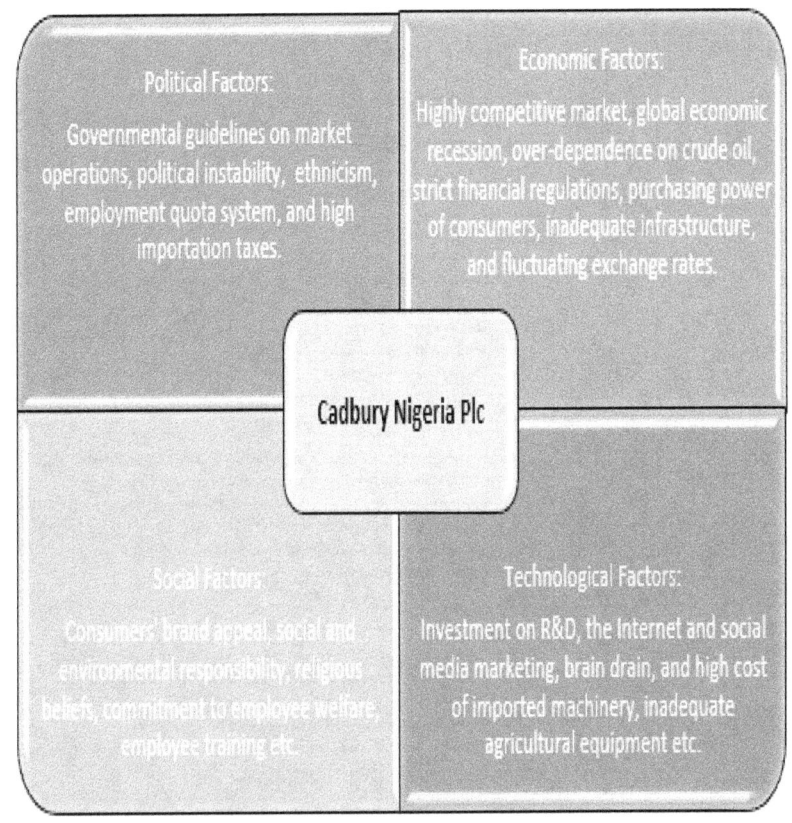

Image 5: PEST Analysis of Cadbury (Concept by Aguilar)

Competitors in the business environment are adapting faster to new dynamic elements which mostly determine an organization's productivity level, profits and competitiveness by altering strategies on pricing and investment (Value Based Management., 2016; Porter., 1985). More explanations are available on Porter's 5 Forces framework in Image 4.

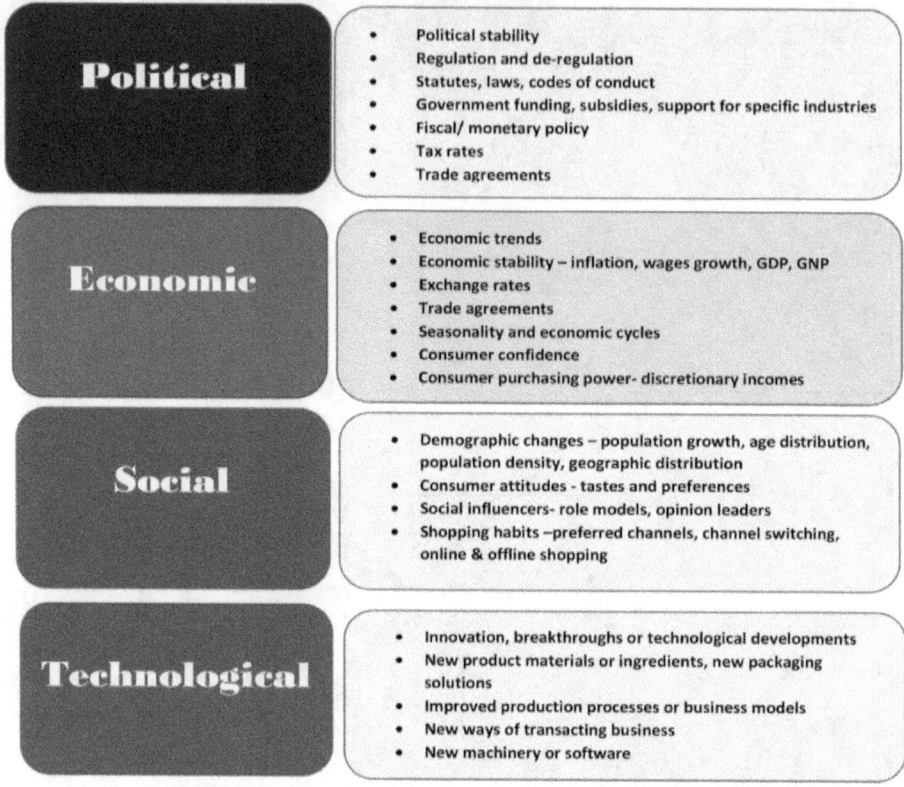

*Image 6: M. E. Porter's 5 Forces Concept*

The analytic model explains Cadbury's competitive business environment, especially its challenges in the scramble to acquire a bigger market share of the food and beverage industry dominated by Nestlé and fiercely contested by other big brands like BUA, UAC, Dangote, CWAY and more. Cadbury's effort to achieve competitiveness, profitability and sustainability through value creation requires optimal use of human and material resources as well as enhanced adaptability to internal and external factors within the business setting. Strategies to be considered here include increased investment in R&D, technology and human capital; highly effective and optimized processes; restructuring of leadership and roles; product differentiation; and unique marketing approaches, among others.

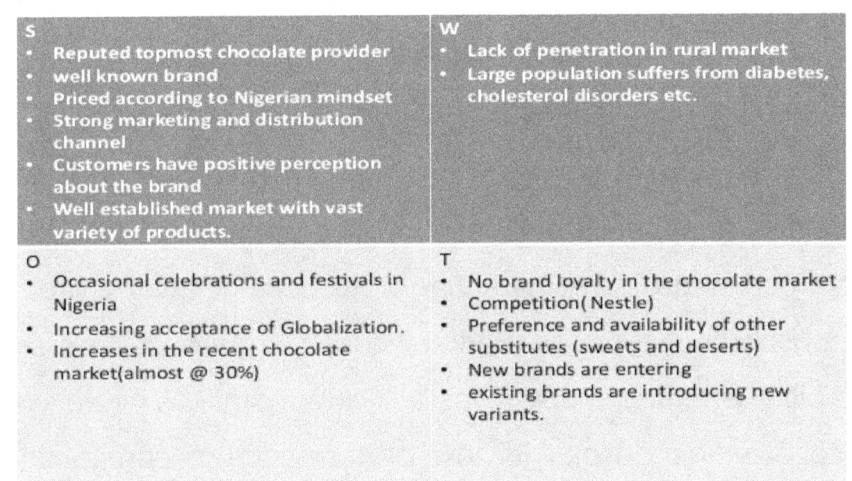

Image 7: M. E. Porter's SWOT Analysis Framework

## 2.4 INNER DYNAMICS

Impact from the 2009 global financial crisis reflects on Cadbury's performance, particularly through high exchange rates, low purchasing power of consumers, and scarcity or incremental price of raw materials. Additionally, the large-scale manufacturer is facing tough challenges from the dilapidated condition of Nigerian roads, including unstable and expensive power supply which increases operational costs due to the exorbitant price of alternative sources of electricity (Murunga, 2022).

To control financial losses, Cadbury has therefore opted for downsizing (Chovwen & Ivensor, 2009). However, government regulations on technological investments have stalled business growth of the manufacturing sector (Okeji, 2019; Sule et al, 2023). The need to cut down operational costs explains Cadbury's 2013 decision on shareholders' excess cash and, more specifically, devaluation of shares value in a period when customers/investors are becoming selective and nearly impossible to please. The shift to imported goods thus makes highlights a need for organizations to embrace aggressive marketing, low pricing, quality products and consumer safety for market visibility, competitiveness and profitability. Strategic innovations by Cadbury makes it relevant on the global stage despite its low performance in comparison to Nestle (Ikyanyon et al, 2020).

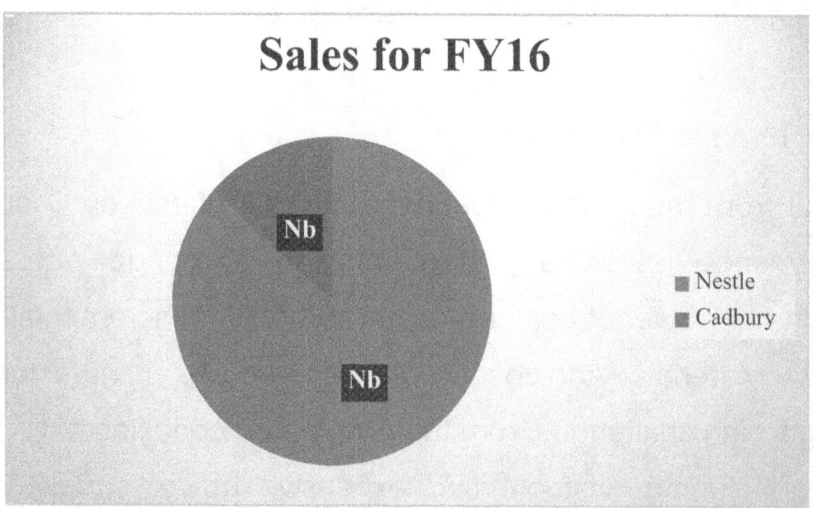

*Image 8: Cadbury vs Nestle Financials for FY16 (Source: 4Traders)*

## 2.5 THE PAYOFF CONCEPT

In Cresswell's 1994 piece, Payoffs refer to every loss incurred, or benefit achieved from organizations' efforts towards improving employee welfare and impacting on the lives of individuals and households in host communities' mainly through effective and strategic corporate social responsibility (CSR) investments (Raimi, 2018; Uduji et al, 2024; Ismail & Tejumaiye, 2022). Payoffs also include expenditures on producing high-value, affordable and safe products/services. Cresswell distinguished payoffs as either quantitative or qualitative (Berridge & Cooper, 1994; Wong et al, 2016).

On this premise, findings show that Cadbury and Nestle have invested heavily on developing its human capital, process and technology for business expansion and sustainable profits notwithstanding obstacles posed by new entrants in the food and beverage manufacturing sector. The image below explains Cadbury's turnover growth rate

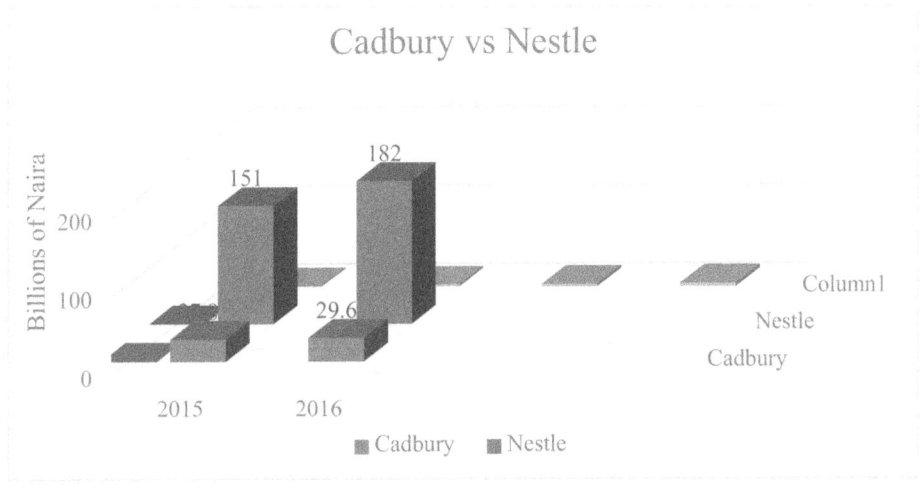

*Image 6: Turnover Growth Rate for FY15 - FY16 (Source: 4Traders)*

Nestle competition against Cadbury for FY16, having documented incremental growth in gross earnings—N151bn (2015) and N182bn (2016). The growth rate of 19.8% was far above Cadbury's meagre N27.8bn (2015) and N29.9 (2016) which was only 7.6%.

## 2.6 Grammar

The financial performance from Cadbury between FY15 and FY16 was rated low in comparison with the giant strides from its biggest competitor, Nestle. However, business analysts argue that the global financial crisis was to blame. Earnings from both companies show how profits can be maximised—even in volatile business environments—through change and innovation strategies. Cadbury therefore needs a policy shift to remain competitive and this requires clear understanding of the company's threats, opportunities, weaknesses and strengths (Beinhocker., 2006; Castelblanco et al, 2024; Le Queux & Peetz, 2013).

## 2.7 Cadbury's Major Threat

Cadbury's major challenge lies in the managers' myopic view of advertising as the newest marketing strategy for capturing value through increased customer base and wider markets.

## 2.8 Solutions from the BSC and SRM

### 2.8.1 The BSC Solution

BSC is very useful in evaluating an organizations' financial performance (past and present), including every change and innovation process or activities that are applied in line with the firm's business objectives and values to achieve growth. This methodology therefore relies on four pivotal aspects vis-a-vis finance, clientele, internal processes, and learning and growth (Hladchenko, 2015; Zahoor & Sahaf, 2018; Chavan, 2009).

From this backdrop, an analysis of Cadbury with the 4-perspective methodology will provide the Consultant with insights into the business environment and, in turn, aid formulation of the most productive, value-creating strategies that guarantee customer/investor satisfaction (Wake, 2015).

Cadbury Nigeria thus need to change from existing business strategy and focus on investments that promote low-cost but effective persuasive advertising. The publicity approach should also aim at downplaying the company's weaknesses while emphasizing on its strengths as a measure for improving earnings, enhancing market visibility and repositioning to compete against Nestle Nigeria from a vantage point (Adeoolu et al, 2015; Akram et al, 2018).

It is also necessary for the manufacturer to strategize towards unifying activities between suppliers, distributors, marketers and end-users. This can be achieved by setting up a responsive feedback channel for consumers' complaints, suggestions and problems. Further, employees of the company should be sensitized on the benefits of such feedback mediums and how to use them effectively for value creation. Consumers show commitment to their organizational roles and responsibilities and are willing to improve their capacity levels when the system does not alienate but include them in the decision-making processes. A clear understanding on the company's mission, core values and beliefs does not only improve employee performance and realization of set goals, but it also enhances processes and create value which is a prerequisite for building a cordial relationship with investors (Marvi et al, 2022; Jaakkola & Alexander, 2024; Roopak & Chakrabarti, 2024

The Consultant hereby suggests that Cadbury should regularly examine its business processes, invest in R&D, and apply innovative advertising to attain organizational goals.

### 2.8.2 Solution through the Strategy Map

Cadbury needs to change its inner dynamics to improve current earnings which fall below Nestle's. Pricing is also another aspect of the competition. Considering the insignificant different between the price of Cadbury's Bournvita and Nestle's Milo, the former has a good chance of dominating the markets if its leadership adapts to strategic innovation. Culture re-orientation is therefore necessary for Cadbury to maximise growth opportunities in the food beverage manufacturing sector.

Investment in technological development is another factor to be considered for Cadbury's resurgence. This will enhance rollout of quality, safe, affordable and differentiated products that appeal to consumers and inspire purchases with less consideration for pricing.

Cadbury's internal business activities, especially on learning and growth, should be reviewed for immediate business transformation. Regular trainings should be organized for suppliers and distributors to enhance their professional levels for excellence—even in previously unknown markets. In furtherance, Cadbury Nigeria should evaluate its operational management approaches and improve processes through bonding of suppliers and distributors in the value chain, considering their roles as well as positive implications of strategic collaborations (Cheung et al, 2024).

Efforts should therefore gear towards low-cost strategies that can significantly increase total tangible and intangible assets, as well as efficient delivery of goods and services to end-users. Reducing cost of production is another measure that guarantees high productivity levels, but the quality of products matters most to consumers, and as such, enhancing the production process as well as eliminating every unproductive activity will sustain value creation and offer maximum benefits to all stakeholders.

According to Spotts et al (2014), other solutions include maximal use of resources, strategic use of working capital, and institutionalization of a responsible management with the capacity to timely implement, monitor and control policy initiatives. Relationship building with suppliers, distributors and consumers is also very important to achieving organizational goals. Use of effective communication channels will not only aid the management in proper handling of issues, suggestions and criticisms, but will also provide a guideline on innovative approaches that strengthen competitive advantage (Wake, 2015; Kurt Christensen, 2010; Zameer et al, 2024).

## 2.9 SUGGESTIONS FOR BUSINESS TRANSFORMATION

Findings from this study show there's no remarkable difference in pricing mechanisms used by both companies: Cadbury and Nestle. The major difference lies in consumers' perception of the brands which are largely influenced by advertising. This indicates Cadbury has the potential to topple competitors through innovative advertising (Barari et al, 2024).

The following suggestions will enhance Cadbury's competitive advantage if properly implemented:

1. **Choice of Advertisers:** The output quality and experience of advertising companies, individuals or media houses play a major role in translating print and electronic media ads into sales and profits. Churchill (1995) suggests that such professional services should come from advertisers who have access to advanced media technologies and data-driven insights on market trends and can formulate effective business strategies in line with local and international standards to influence consumers' buying preference and help clients/brands to achieve sustainable competitive advantage.

2. **Brand Enhancement:** The bottom line of advertising is brand enhancement, which distinguishes companies, products and

services available in marketplace. Brand enhancement is one of the reasons consumers remain loyal to some brands no matter the cost difference when compared to competitors. Companies enhance their brands by combining persuasive advertising with consistent delivery of high-quality and valuable goods and services.

3. **Innovative Advertising:** Cadbury needs change and innovation strategies in its business model, particularly advertising choices. The company should consider using highly educative ideas such as comparing its products with similar goods in a way that those competing products or companies are not mentioned but implied in the message. Li et al (2002) noted that consumers are mostly inquisitive about convincing claims and can easily switch once expectations are met.

4. **Suppliers and Distributors:** Cadbury must improve its supply chain by hiring experienced workers and investing in human capital development to increase employee motivation, engagement, and job satisfaction. Regular training events will not only improve productivity levels but also foster long-term relationships between the company and its customers. Considering that distributors and suppliers also gather meaningful information from the markets which are subsequently applied in decision-making processes, Cadbury should implement solid relationship-building programs/policies that value suppliers and distributors as part of the value chain.

## 2.10 Risks of Neglecting the Proposals

Findings from the recent decline in sales and profits show that Cadbury has underused its potentials. According to Okigbo (1997), companies need persuasive advertising to remain visible in the markets, expand markets and increase profits. If Cadbury management fails to strictly adhere to proposals in this study, here are a few consequences it might encounter:

a. The company will lose a large part of its market share to Nestle and other fast-growing contenders in the manufacturing sector.

b. Low performance will lead to undercapitalization and an eventual collapse.

c. Nestle will monopolize the food beverage manufacturing sector and thereby dictating prices in its favour as other less competitive companies opt for closure.

d. Affected workers at Cadbury will be thrown out of the working class and as such lose their purchasing power. This, in turn, affect the national economic growth indicators.

e. Many skilled personnel will migrate to rival companies and sell out intellectual property acquired from years of experience at Cadbury.

f. Affected workers or unions may file lawsuits against Cadbury for breaching contractual agreements thereby increasing the total amount of losses incurred by the manufacturer.

## 2.11 Consultant's Opinion and Advice

Cadbury Nigeria Plc understands effective communication as the motive of advertising, but the problem lies with understanding what customers crave for, knowing what ads are suitable for which medium or age group, and considering the time and place for action. No matter the chosen platform, advertising must be dramatic, appealing, bold, convincing and persuasive.

Based on findings from this study, Cadbury needs more investments in training its marketers and upgrading their welfare packages. Similarly, the company should actively participate in community projects through life-changing investments in CSR and social or environmental responsibility.

Apart from adapting to strategies that link up the company and its customers, Cadbury management should maximise use of responsive websites that allow seamless online payments, effective dissemination of information, provision of after-sales service, and submission of queries, complaints, or suggestions. This includes timely delivery of purchased goods in good condition to customers' homes. Where necessary, buyers should have extra benefits, especially for repeated buys—if the company wants to generate sales leads (Chen & Lee., 2005).

Choice of advertising mediums or methods is crucial for business survival, and Cadbury must identify and collaborate with the best advertisers (brand marketers) to achieve the desired ads impact on existing or potential buyers. The company should also conduct private assessment on the performance of advertising, with regards to turnover, to ascertain whether it should be eliminated or adjusted. Continuous advertising is therefore necessary for a product's longevity. This requires regular evaluations and adaptations to changing needs in today's complex, volatile, and constantly evolving markets.

Lastly, Cadbury should integrate effective change and innovation strategies that support value-based management practices. It is equally necessary to enhance the management process, restructure leadership (especially where change to resistance is noticed or expected), and conduct regular reviews of policies, business activities, and performance for proper adjustments that align with organizational mission, values, and objectives in ways that enhance brand image. The Consultant is certain that strict adherence to these suggestions will improve efficiency (Baker., 1996).

# Chapter 3

## Evidence Review

### 3.0 Introduction to Advertising

The continuous decline in resources and competitiveness has promoted managers in different industries to consider implementing changes in their business models/processes and improve the quality of goods or services offered to consumers in local and global markets (Brannemo., 2006; Adjei et al, 2024; Angela Chang & Kukar-Kinney, 2011; Gurley et al, 2005). This highlights the need for outsourcing, a management strategy that encourages organizations to delegate various key activities to professionals/specialists who have track records in delivering maximum quality (Cousins et al., 2006; Cengiz et al, 2024). Advertisers are a key element in marketing/sales planning. They also play crucial roles in brand enhancement, revenue performance, and market expansion because people enjoy watching attractive, educative and entertaining ads even when they have no clear perspective of what advertising signifies. Osanlou & Rezaei (2024) noted that the love for quality adverts is evident in the fact that viewers, especially in the electronic media, fail to notice the interruptions during popular television programmes or sports events when such adverts are displayed. McNeill (2013) pointed out that aggressive advertising is a common place in digital media while Liu et al (2023) added that people only get tired of viewing the less appealing or non-innovative ones. Other scholars agree that advertising mediums are found everywhere—in the offices, homes, streets, print and electronic media, among others (Adeolu et al, 2005; Michaelidou et al, 2021; Gebreselassie & Bougie, 2019).

Onunkwo (1997) and Terrence (2007) defined advertising as a paid, strategic marketing plan through which consumers get information about the benefits they can gain from using products/services from certain brands. The aim of this practice is to arouse inquisitiveness that leads to immediate or future purchase. Advertising is therefore a means of creating awareness for goods and services, with sales and profits as the interior motives when properly utilized (Shi et al, 2022; Lahtinen et al, 2020).

No company survives without a form of advertising—paid or free. In addition, persuasive advertising can never be effective if it has no direct impact on consumers' preferences (Chen, 2018).

According to Shi et al (2022), the impact of advertising on consumer choices is never clear unless the message from a particular company triggers significant rise in sales performance of a specified product or service. Lahtinen et al (2020) noted that the purpose of advertising is to distinguish goods from different brands. Barnard and Chen (2018) however discredited advertising as an innovative marketing tool because it fails to recognize the negative effects of using harmful products or services such as cigarettes, caffeinated drinks, canned foods, sugary foods and more. On the other hand, various scholars argue that advertising is undervalued despite its contributions to the growth of businesses and world economies (Giakoumaki et al, 2016; Diehl et al, 2007; De Meulenaer et al, 2015).

## 3.1 THE STRATEGY ROAD MAP METHODOLOGY

There's a relationship between sales, profits and advertising, and these are all foundational to the success of organizations. The strategic road map (SRM) thus seeks to understand the determining factors between a business strategy and branding, as well as how both collaborate to improve earnings (Baaij & Reinmoeller, 2018; Carlos et al, 2018)

Further, advertising is a key aspect of productivity; it increases sales volume and ultimately boosts overall profits. In Nigeria, advertisers rely on cultural values whereas their Western counterparts focus on market-oriented ads. However, media advertising has been criticized for distorting facts, especially on the economic, political, and socio-cultural development indicators of growing economies. Business leaders can however address these shortcomings by implementing industry- and/or country-specific strategies that align with change and innovation models (Spotts et al, 2014; Demunter & Bauwens, 2023).

### 3.1.1 STRATEGY

In business, administration entails planning, directing, controlling, budgeting and renumeration. The marketing mix of product, place, promotion and price are also adapted to the to attain organizational goals. However, according to Chesbrough and Rosenbloom (2002), successful companies are those that maximise opportunities provided by the concepts to improve sales volume, decrease operational costs and increase profits. Managers must therefore understand that strategies are the key to business survival, and that business models are most productive when change and innovation are infused in branding and advertising. This continuously creates value for stakeholders in any profit-oriented system.

Spotts et al (2014) explains that strategy is a streamlined, comprehensive and easy-to-use plan which individuals, groups, organizations and governmental bodies integrate to achieve sustainable competitive advantage over market contenders as well as to reduce or eliminate the impact of internal and external factors within the business environment. When properly applied, and in line with organizational vales, goals and aspirations, strategies become essential value drivers which managers should constantly review and update for sustainable growth. Baaij and Reinmoeller (2018) on the other hand viewed strategies as lines of action through which organizations different product and services to create value for shareholders while adequately compensating the society with commitment to improving development indicators, and offering quality benefits to customers who patronize their products and services.

Further, Carlos et al (2018) contradicted previous opinions on the purpose of business strategy. The scholars argued that an effective management or the process of achieving business growth depends on whether employees support organizational objectives/values/policies, and how they understand their job responsibilities and work process as well as the efficiency of links between management and staff across all departments. This explains why investment in human capital is crucial in building resilience, strengthening efficiency, and achieving sustainable competitive advantage. Again, Carlos et al (2018) suggested performance appraisal and monitoring of activities to adjust or eliminate unproductive processes.

Landaeta Olivo et al (2016) explained that the relationship between effective advertising enhances a firm's understanding or closeness to its customers. De Meulenaer et al (2015) opined that advertising is most productive when elements of timing, operational activities, planning, control and supervision are maximised in line with the company's budget and business objectives. Diehl et al (2007) also argued that there is no significant difference between advertising and marketing, adding that both concepts provide organizations with far-reaching information dissemination outlets that expand target markets and increase profits.

SRM and BSC highlight the existing interrelatedness between organizational structures and how business leaders maximize assets (tangible and intangible) (Baaij & Reinmoeller, 2018). Both management approaches aid understanding of workers' opinion about strategic management, innovative leadership, employee performance, organizational goals, and business process (Zameer et al, 2024). Additionally, the tools serve as a measurement framework through which contributions from distributors, suppliers and marketers are weighted to validate results that are subsequently used in financial planning.

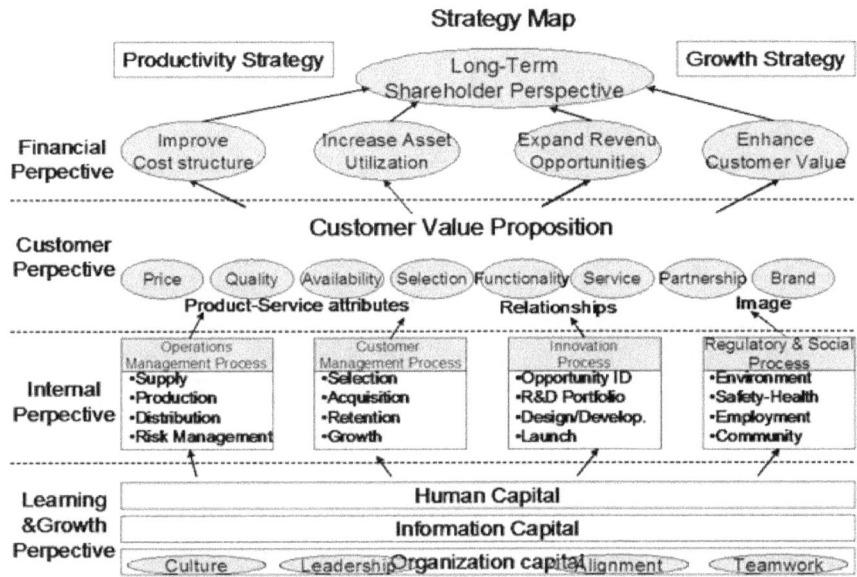

Image 7: Kaplan and Norton's Concept of SRM

Kaplan and Norton are of the opinion that SRM helps users in assessing the links between assets, with focus is however on value creation and sustainable growth. The BSC and SRM standards are as follows:

- To create great value through improved internal business processes.

- To offer unique products and services that perfectly suit consumer needs. This is considered as the main aspect of creating value.

- To adjust antagonistic elements of short-term financial goals to reduce price and, at the same time, expand profits.

- To define organizational values, especially on what are considered as intangible resources and those that should be aligned with human capital, information, as well as learning and growth perspective.

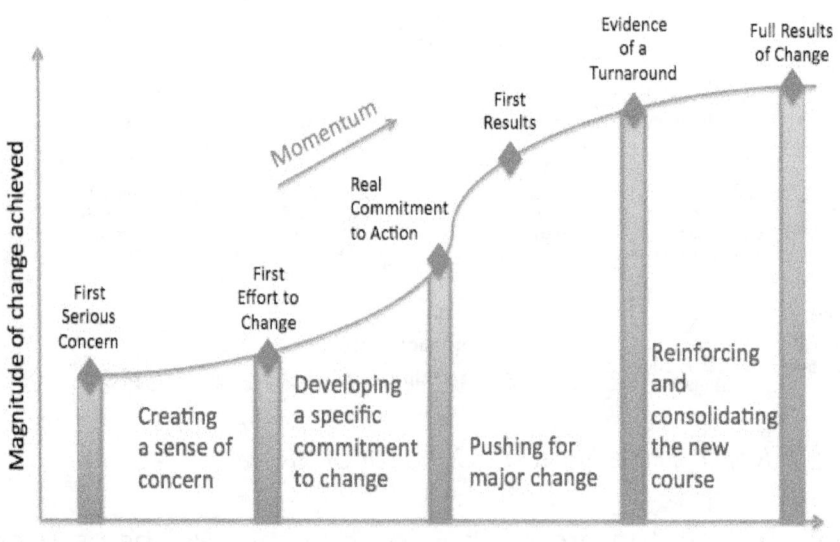

Image 8: Eden and Ackerman's 5-stage SRM

## 3.2 BENEFITS OF STRATEGY ROADMAP

SRM is a strategy adapted by organizations to enhance the production process as well as increase productivity levels, employee welfare, managerial output, and earnings from effective advertisement on print and electronic media. Other benefits of the strategy roadmap are as follows:

- Optimised communication links in the value chain, including private organizations.

- Improved evaluation procedures that ease understanding of organizations' market performance.

- Better knowledge of organizational values, objectives and standards by employees.

- Strengthened goals that influence market visibility through unique approaches.

- Emphasis on cash, timing and capabilities of actors in the system and maximization of these factors for business growth.

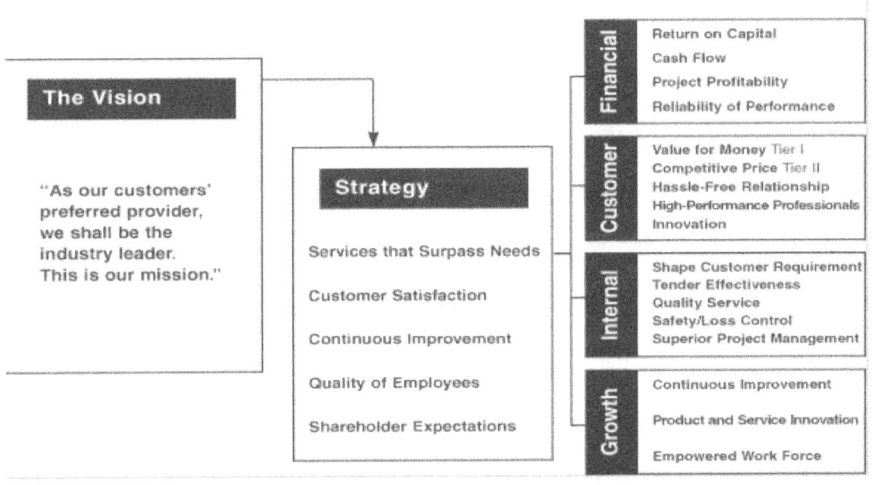

Image 9: Meryer and Allen's Framework on Strategic Objectives

## 3.3 Planning with SRM

BSC and SRM exist for the sole purpose of distinguishing brands from their market challengers through the identification of each organizations internal processes or activities, including the value and functions of assets (tangible or intangible) that provide competitiveness.

## 3.4 Implementing and Updating the Strategy Map

According to Cheung et al (2024), every organization needs a strategic plan and performance assessment mechanisms that differentiate productive and unproductive activities. The design also identifies problem areas within companies, suggests the appropriate time and how SRM and BSC are applied, as well as indicates the periodic review process that enhance market dominance.

Roopak and Chakrabarti (2024) also suggest that organizations should regularly evaluate activities to ensure optimal performance and sustainable growth, adding that managers and executives should always integrate SRM and BSC tools as guides for taking decisions and planning future activities. The management approaches, however, are flawed because they do not emphasize providing explanations to the affected individuals and groups involved in business activities (Fallahi Daryakenari et al, 2024).

## 3.5 SRM Limitations

Martins (2013) adds that SRM failed for as a strategic management tool for its inability to categorically explain organizational activities and what purposes they stand for. This indicates that SRM does not rely on assumptions to question the rationale behind any activity, process or need.

## 3.6 The Balanced Score Card (BSC) Methodology

Kaplan and Norton found through their 2005 study that successful organizations are those whose leaders regularly conduct analysis of business situations, particularly in the monetary aspect, and with the use of essential evaluation tools such as customers, internal activities/process as well as learning and development.

On this premise, Marvi et al (2022) concluded that the purpose for which any organization exists is found in its mission statement and plans. The scholars added that managers must check performance to ensure compliance with the objectives, vision, and mission of organizations, and where necessary, apply innovative ideas and/or effective remedies. This methodology is widely used in the 21st century because it focuses on the development of internal processes and evaluation of how intangible assets enhance or impede growth of businesses.

Additionally, companies differ in management and practice, yet the role of BSC as a major pathway through which best value-creating strategies are examined, changed, or eliminated.

BSC delves into organizational activities, concepts, ideas and aspirations to provide management with clear understanding of performance levels. It also distinguishes between productive and unproductive activities. As a strategic management tool, BSC supports adaptation to a streamlined strategy and clear vision through which activities are controlled for high profits, value creation and sustainability. Kaplan and Norton described the framework as a reliable tool that stabilizes a firm's strategies and processes (Kurt Christensen, 2010).

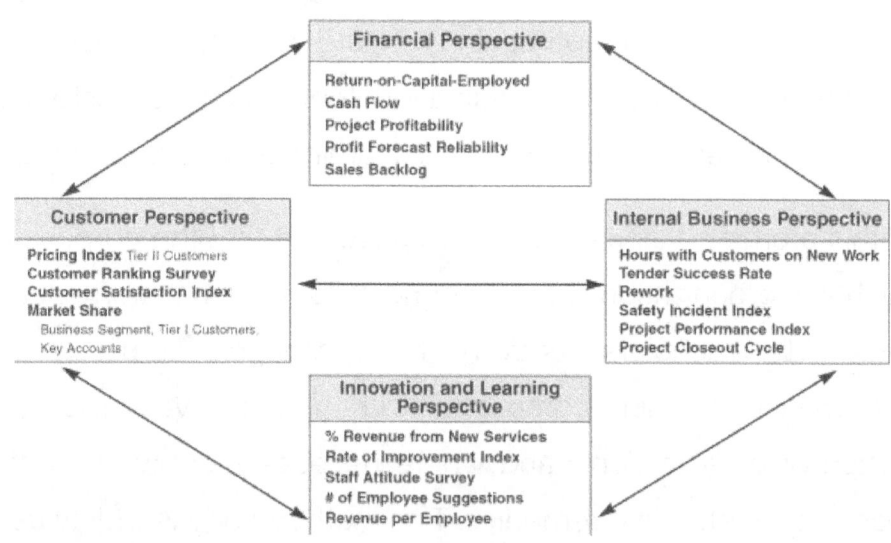

*Image 10: Kaplan and Norton's BSC Concept*

BSC's performance assessment metrics are error-free, and they provide organizations with workable solutions to all problems in structure, process and use of resources. It also provides answers to myriads of questions about the organization's strengths, weaknesses, opportunities and threats. Developing this strategy-reliant model, however, entails having a perfect understanding of the company's structure and careful implementation of strategies.

## 3.7 BSC AS A MANAGEMENT SYSTEM

Most organizations conduct their businesses with performance assessment frameworks that provide fiscal and nonfinancial calculations, but BSC is different, unique, and the most common estimation tool. Progressive companies therefore apply change and innovation strategies through the scorecard, which serves as a major check on the administrative process.

The Consultant therefore suggests that Cadbury management should first choose a simple, realistic and less cumbersome scorecard that inspires unity of purpose. This plan of action must be thoroughly explained to workers across all departments (business units) to achieve the desired results. Importantly, BSC users cannot achieve their objectives unless they change their perspective of the BSC concept as a measurement tool to a dynamic management model upon which innovative leaders achieve sustainable competitive advantage for their organizations.

## 3.8 DO COMPANIES NEED A BSC?

Since this 21$^{st}$ century, business enterprises have operated in volatile environments which emphasize the need for effective assessment tools and use of aggressive advertising to boost sales, marketing and profits. To achieve organizational growth, managers are now looking up to media analysts and increasing investments in consumer-based ideas that maximise companies' strengths. These strategies will not achieve their purposes without use of financial performance evaluation frameworks (Roopak & Chakrabarti, 2024).

The Balanced Score Card uses financial calculations to determine the productivity level of top management staff, employees, suppliers and distributors, advertisers, and other players in the value chain. However, BSC capacity to use more integrated and broad assessment structure in linking finance, customers and internal process, and ascertain system performance for both short and long-term investments, makes the management tool appealing to most managers. Fallahi Daryakenari et al (2024) explained that BSC helps users to identify unproductive activities or processes within an organization. It also highlights areas that need adjustment. In addition, BSC provides managers with the most suitable options they should integrate in the management structure to boost performance.

## 3.9 Prospective DBA Perspective for Transforming Clients' Business

Current trends in global businesses highlight the need for competitive advantage and this is worrisome to most policymakers and economists in developing economies because some external factors such as capital, politics, infrastructure development, among others, are discouraging potential large-scale entrepreneurs as well as scaring off foreign and local investors. Nigeria's manufacturing industry has been a major contributor to National Income (NI) and has more to offer in the nation's economic diversification objectives. The government's diversification strategy has also repositioned agriculture and Small and Medium-scale Enterprises (SMEs) which serve as growth drivers for food and beverage manufacturers like Cadbury. Additionally, products from the company are considered appealing to buyers in global markets but there's a need for more investments in advertising. A strong presence in the media will not only reposition the company's stand against competitors but offer a chance to outpace Nestle in Nigeria's food and beverage manufacturing sector.

Effective advertising is therefore invaluable to any organization's quest to convert consumers and increase sales volume for more profits. On this premise, I look forward to conducting advanced research on "The Impact of Advertising on the Growth of Nigerian SMEs." I am optimistic that results from the study will enhance entrepreneurship development in the country, provide more jobs, enhance equitable distribution of wealth, and contribute to Nigeria's economic growth strategies.

# Chapter 4

## An Assessment of the Researcher's Employability Enhancement

### 4.1 Personal Qualities Required to Successfully Complete this Assignment

To conduct this research like a professional in the real world, I had to gain composure since objectivity was essential to arrive at valid conclusions.

The study shows that a major problem with Nigeria companies, not just the strength of competitors in Nigeria's food and beverage; other key factors include lack of commitment to relationship-building strategies and poor investment in advertising, which has the capacity to transform businesses in both short and long terms. The study module for this coursework will be useful in my future educational and career pursuits and lessons learned will certainly boost my performance at the global stage.

The acquired knowledge and practical skills have significantly improved my competence as a research student. Most importantly, learning how to successfully apply PEST analysis, SWOT and the Meta model on a company has expanded my idea of strategic management as well as increased my capacity to transform an organization's weakness into strength. I am pleased with the results from this research although some identified weaknesses highlight the need for personal advancement in my future academic endeavours.

## 4.2 Evaluation of the Researcher's Ability for this Academic Task

Before starting the model and completing this coursework, I had limited knowledge of the analytic frameworks applied in this research. The theme was intimidating and confusing at the start however, discussions I had with the tutor gave me an insight. It is a thing of joy to know that at the end, I have succeeded in analysing business operations of a company with regards to advertising, sales, and profits.  Further, gaining full knowledge of an organization's current market position, competitors, history, policies, legal provisions and regulatory framework through analytical frameworks like the Meta model is highly encouraging.

I gained deep insights into previously unfamiliar methodologies, concepts, and relevant studies in business management. In the end, my idea of project designing and execution as well as the time factor in conducting quality, reliable and effective consultancy services has gained significant boost. Moreover, I now have better understanding of how organizations evaluate performance according to the four-phase perspectives of financial, internal business processes, customer, and innovation and learning.

Notably, I learned of the importance of a well-structured BSC and how the methodology determines a company's profitability, growth and sustainability. In continuation, a comprehensive evaluation of this module gave me an opportunity to make application of the SRM as a solution-finder to several circumstantial challenges that reduce customer satisfaction and engagement as well as hamper value creation for stakeholders.

I am elated to have acquired knowledge of a powerful Nigeria-based multinational company, particularly Cadbury's growth and sustenance secrets in the areas of (a) leadership competence (b) quality delivery of goods and services, and (c) use of effective, dynamic and suitable marketing strategies to increase business performance in a competitive market environment.

Lastly, I am aware of the lasting benefits of innovative leadership and a culture that promotes creativity, collaboration, diversity, inclusion, and agility. Successful leaders, in my opinion, are those who influence strategy design processes and control implementation in line with organizational goals which revolve around creating value for stakeholders and consistently improving customer experience.

## 4.3 Related Leadership Skills needed for Personal Development and Career Growth

From this task, I now have a different, constructive perspective about on business. I believe this understanding will bring to bear a lifetime impact as I continue to develop my competence level in preparation for the world stage.

Though I am currently taking management courses, the understanding I have about the rigours of business management in both theory and practice was low. Yet I learned so much from this module, for example, studies indicate no organization survives competition without investing in research and development (R&D), talent/process development, and effective—or sometimes aggressive—marketing techniques. It is thus understandable why advertising is an indispensable part of SRM. This module also broadened my perspective on how organizations create value via regular training and by ensuring employees have a clear understanding of organizational objectives, business strategies, and job responsibilities.

Completion of this coursework requires good time-management abilities, with focus on effective delivery of services and timing of ads in real world business settings where professionals and consultants have a responsibility of providing value for money within a timeframe. "Time," they say, "is money." Therefore, it is a vital feature for all successful enterprises.

Despite some challenges, I have the courage to advance my study and career with achievements from completing this academic research, particularly how to control frustrations encountered while analysing business models and strategy to identify a plan that best guarantees quality delivery of goods and services to all stakeholders.

Another important leadership skill gained from the module is SRM, gives business leaders a direction for expected short- and long-term results. I hope to practicalize the knowledge and skills on future modules, particularly my upcoming PhD research which evaluates my capability as a senior executive who oversees the decision-making process of an organization. This, I believe, will boost my readiness to face business innovation and strategic management challenges at the global stage.

It is true that managers should have the competence to design effective—and maybe new—strategies to achieve sustainable competitive advantage against market rivals. Hence, I am eager to acquire innovative leadership skills and business acumen required to drive growth in organizations throughout my professional career.

# REFERENCES

Adeolu B. Ayanwale, Taiwo Alimi and Matthew A. Ayanbimipe (2005). The Influence of Advertising on Consumer Brand Preference. Journal of Social Sciences, 10(1): 9-16.

Adjei, A.A.F., Gatsi, J.G., Owusu Appiah, M., Abeka, M.J. and Owusu Junior, P. (2024), "Financial globalization, governance and economic growth in Sub-Saharan Africa", Journal of Financial Economic Policy, Vol. ahead-of-print No. ahead-of-print.

Ahlqvist, T., Bäck, A., Heinonen, S. and Halonen, M. (2010), "Road-mapping the societal transformation potential of social media", Foresight, Vol. 12 No. 5, pp. 3-26.

Akram, U., Hui, P., Kaleem Khan, M., Tanveer, Y., Mehmood, K. and Ahmad, W. (2018), "How website quality affects online impulse buying: Moderating effects of sales promotion and credit card use", Asia Pacific Journal of Marketing and Logistics, Vol. 30 No. 1, pp. 235-256.

Angela Chang, C. and Kukar-Kinney, M. (2011), "The effects of shopping aid usage on consumer purchase decision and decision satisfaction", Asia Pacific Journal of Marketing and Logistics, Vol. 23 No. 5, pp. 745-754.

Baaij, M. and Reinmoeller, P. (2018), "Making Your Strategy Work: Anticipating Execution Issues", Mapping a Winning Strategy: Developing and Executing a Successful Strategy in Turbulent Markets, Emerald Publishing Limited, Leeds, pp. 139-171.

Baoku, L., Cuixia, Z. and Weimin, B. (2010), "An empirical study on the decision-making styles of the Chinese peasant consumers", Journal of Consumer Marketing, Vol. 27 No. 7, pp. 629-637.

Barari, M., Ross, M., Quach, S. and Surachartkumtonkun, J. (2024), "Using text and image mining to study how actor engagement creates value in the sharing economy", European Journal of Marketing, Vol. ahead-of-print No. ahead-of-print.

Berridge, J.R. and Cooper, C.L. (1994), "The Employee Assistance Programme: Its Role in Organizational Coping and Excellence", Personnel Review, Vol. 23 No. 7, pp. 4-20.

Binci, D., Cerruti, C. and Braganza, A. (2016), "Do vertical and shared leadership need each other in change management?", Leadership & Organization Development Journal, Vol. 37 No. 5, pp. 558-578.

Carlos, R., Amaral, D.C. and Caetano, M. (2018), "Framework for continuous agile technology roadmap updating", Innovation & Management Review, Vol. 15 No. 3, pp. 321-336.

Castelblanco, G., Guevara, J. and De Marco, A. (2024), "Crisis management in public–private partnerships: lessons from the global crises in the XXI century", Built Environment Project and Asset Management, Vol. 14 No. 1, pp. 56-73.

Cengiz, H., Gokce Arpa, R. and Sezgin, K.N. (2024), "Appearance vanity or achievement vanity: which better predicts young consumers' decision-making orientations?", Young Consumers, Vol. ahead-of-print No. ahead-of-print.

Chavan, M. (2009), "The balanced scorecard: a new challenge", Journal of Management Development, Vol. 28 No. 5, pp. 393-406.

Chen, H.-J. (2018), "What drives consumers' mobile shopping? 4Ps or shopping preferences?", Asia Pacific Journal of Marketing and Logistics, Vol. 30 No. 4, pp. 797-815.

Cheung, M.L., Leung, W.K.S., Chang, L.M.K., Aw, E.C.-X. and Wong, R.Y.M. (2024), "Immersive time in the metaverse and visits to the physical world: why not both? A holistic customer engagement framework", International Journal of Contemporary Hospitality Management, Vol. ahead-of-print No. ahead-of-print.

Chovwen, C. and Ivensor, E. (2009), "Job insecurity and motivation among women in Nigerian consolidated banks", Gender in Management, Vol. 24 No. 5, pp. 316-326.

Cormier, D., Demaria, S. and Magnan, M. (2017), "Beyond earnings: do EBITDA reporting and governance matter for market participants?", Managerial Finance, Vol. 43 No. 2, pp. 193-211.

De Meulenaer, S., Dens, N. and De Pelsmacker, P. (2015), "Which cues cause consumers to perceive brands as more global? A conjoint analysis", International Marketing Review, Vol. 32 No. 6, pp. 606-626.

Demunter, R. and Bauwens, J. (2023), "Going all the way? LGBTQ people's receptiveness to gay-themed advertising in a Belgian context", European Journal of Marketing, Vol. 57 No. 4, pp. 1219-1241.

Diehl, S., Mueller, B. and Terlutter, R. (2007), "Skepticism Toward Pharmaceutical Advertising in the U.S. and Germany", Taylor, C.R. and Lee, D.-H. (Ed.) Cross-Cultural Buyer Behaviour (Advances in International Marketing, Vol. 18), Emerald Group Publishing Limited, Leeds, pp. 31-60.

Fallahi Daryakenari, N., Jalilvand, M.R. and Jafari, S.M. (2024), "A roadmap of retargeting campaigns for SMEs: a case study", Marketing Intelligence & Planning, Vol. ahead-of-print No. ahead-of-print.

Ferber, J., & Gutknecht, O. (1998). A meta-model for the analysis and design of organizations in multi-agent systems. Proceedings International Conference on Multi Agent Systems (Cat. No.98EX160), 128-135.

Gebreselassie, A.W. and Bougie, R. (2019), "Increasing the effectiveness of advertisements targeting social issues in least developed countries", Journal of Social Marketing, Vol. 9 No. 2, pp. 225-251.

Giakoumaki, C., Avlonitis, G.J. and Baltas, G. (2016), "Does ingredient advertising work? Some evidence on its impact", Journal of Business & Industrial Marketing, Vol. 31 No. 7, pp. 901-913.

Guedes, M.J., Fernandes Crespo, N. and Patel, P.C. (2023), "When in Rome, do as the Romans do: can international marketing adaptation improve the association between sterilization and profitability?", Journal of Business & Industrial Marketing, Vol. 38 No. 10, pp. 2197-2219.

Gurley, T., Lin, S. and Ballou, S. (2005), "Consumer decision process modelling: how leaders can better understand buyers' choices", Strategy & Leadership, Vol. 33 No. 3, pp. 30-40.

Hladchenko, M. (2015), "Balanced Scorecard – a strategic management system of the higher education institution", International Journal of Educational Management, Vol. 29 No. 2, pp. 167-176.

Huang, G. (2019), "Variation matters: How to curb ad intrusiveness for native advertising on Facebook, Twitter, and Instagram", Internet Research, Vol. 29 No. 6, pp. 1469-1484.

Ikyanyon, D., Johnson, P. and Dawson, J. (2020), "Institutional context and human resource management in Nigeria", Employee Relations, Vol. 42 No. 1, pp. 1-16.

Iqbal Anjum, M. (2008), "Islamic world's development policy responses to the challenges of financial globalization", Humanomics, Vol. 24 No. 1, pp. 5-16.

Ismail, F.O. and Tejumaiye, J.A. (2022), "Sociology of tribalism for inclusive corporate social responsibility communication in Nigeria", Corporate Communications: An International Journal, Vol. 27 No. 3, pp. 470-493.

Jaakkola, E. and Alexander, M. (2024), "Understanding and managing engagement journeys", Journal of Service Management, Vol. 35 No. 3, pp. 357-380.

Kotler, Philip. (1980). Marketing Management: Analysis, Planning and Control (4th Edition). United States of America: Prentice Hall Inc..

Kurt Christensen, H. (2010), "Defining customer value as the driver of competitive advantage", Strategy & Leadership, Vol. 38 No. 5, pp. 20-25.

Lahtinen, V., Dietrich, T. and Rundle-Thiele, S. (2020), "Long live the marketing mix. Testing the effectiveness of the commercial marketing mix in a social marketing context", Journal of Social Marketing, Vol. 10 No. 3, pp. 357-375.

Landaeta Olivo, J.F., García Guzmán, J., Colomo-Palacios, R. and Stantchev, V. (2016), "IT innovation strategy: managing the implementation communication and its generated knowledge through the use of an ICT tool", Journal of Knowledge Management, Vol. 20 No. 3, pp. 512-533.

Le Queux, S. and Peetz, D. (2013), "Between "too big to fail" and "too small to matter": The borderless financial crisis and unions", International Journal of Manpower, Vol. 34 No. 3, pp. 198-212.

Li, J., Yu, Y., Liu, C. and Deng, X. (2023), "An optimal strategy of advertising and electronic word-of-mouth with considering rebates", Kybernetes, Vol. 52 No. 12, pp. 6440-6466.

Lin, W., Wang, Y., Samara, G. and Lu, J. (2024), "Governance of corporate social responsibility: a platform ecosystem perspective", Management Decision, Vol. ahead-of-print No. ahead-of-print.

Liu, Y., Zheng, H., Yang, S. and Wang, J. (2023), "How pop-ups drive online sales: moderating effects of online promotions", European Journal of Marketing, Vol. 57 No. 8, pp. 2112-2141.

Marvi, R., Hollebeek, L.D. and Foroudi, P. (2022), "Mapping Customer Engagement's Intellectual: A Multi-Method Bibliometric Approach and Future Directions", Foroudi, P., Nguyen, B. and Melewar, T.C. (Ed.) The Emerald Handbook of Multi-Stakeholder Communication, Emerald Publishing Limited, Leeds, pp. 393-432.

Matthews, L.M. (2017). Applying Multigroup Analysis in PLS-SEM: A Step-by-Step Process.

McNeill, L. (2013), "Sales promotion in Asia: successful strategies for Singapore and Malaysia", Asia Pacific Journal of Marketing and Logistics, Vol. 25 No. 1, pp. 48-69.

Michaelidou, N., Micevski, M. and Halkias, G. (2021), "How do international advertisers use consumer culture positioning strategies? A cross-national, cross-category approach", International Marketing Review, Vol. 38 No. 2, pp. 367-386.

Munir, K. and Bukhari, M. (2020), "Impact of globalization on income inequality in Asian emerging economies", International Journal of Sociology and Social Policy, Vol. 40 No. 1/2, pp. 44-57.

Murunga, P. (2022), "An Anecdotal Examination of Corporate Social Responsibility Through an African Eye. The Kenyan Experiences", Ogunyemi, K., Ogunyemi, O. and Anozie, A. (Ed.) Responsible Management in Africa, Volume 2: Ethical Work and Sustainability, Emerald Publishing Limited, Leeds, pp. 51-66.

Okeji, C.C. (2019), "Research output of librarians in the field of library and information science in Nigeria: a bibliometric analysis from 2000-March, 2018", Collection and Curation, Vol. 38 No. 3, pp. 53-60.

Omar Trejo-Pech, C., Weldon, R.N. and House, L.A. (2008), "Earnings, accruals, cash flows, and EBITDA for agribusiness firms", Agricultural Finance Review, Vol. 68 No. 2, pp. 301-319.

Osanlou, B. and Rezaei, E. (2024), "The effect of Muslim consumers' religiosity on brand verdict", Journal of Islamic Marketing, Vol. ahead-of-print No. ahead-of-print.

Otusanya, O.J., Liu, J. and Lauwo, S.G. (2023), "Influence of tax dodging on tax justice in developing countries: some theory and evidence from Sub-Saharan Africa", Journal of Financial Crime, Vol. 30 No. 2, pp. 332-360.

Raimi, L. (2018), "Reinventing CSR in Nigeria: Understanding Its Meaning and Theories for Effective Application in the Industry", Redefining Corporate Social Responsibility (Developments in Corporate Governance and Responsibility, Vol. 13), Emerald Publishing Limited, Leeds, pp. 143-176.

Roopak, R. and Chakrabarti, S. (2024), "Framing knowledge structure of customer engagement: a multimethod review", VINE Journal of Information and Knowledge Management Systems, Vol. ahead-of-print No. ahead-of-print.

Russo, D., Ciancarini, P., Falasconi, T., & Tomasi, M. (2018). A Meta-Model for Information Systems Quality. ACM Transactions on Management Information Systems (TMIS), 9, 1 - 38.

Shi, D., Zhang, W., Zou, G. and Ping, J. (2022), "Advertising and pricing strategies for the manufacturer in the presence of brown and green products", Kybernetes, Vol. 51 No. 4, pp. 1452-1477.

Sokolova, A. and Vishnevskiy, K. (2023), "An integrated approach for the evaluation of corporate foresight: the example of a Russian corporation", Foresight, Vol. 25 No. 3, pp. 305-319.

Spotts, E.H., Weinberger, G.M. and Weinberger, F.M. (2014), "Publicity and advertising: what matter most for sales?", European Journal of Marketing, Vol. 48 No. 11/12, pp. 1986-2008.

Sule, B., Sambo, U. and Yusuf, M. (2023), "Countering cybercrimes as the strategy of enhancing sustainable digital economy in Nigeria", Journal of Financial Crime, Vol. 30 No. 6, pp. 1557-1574.

Tan, Y., Zhou, H., Wu, P. and Huang, L. (2023), "The optimal carbon emission reduction and advertising strategy with dynamic market share in the supply chain", Industrial Management & Data Systems, Vol. 123 No. 10, pp. 2435-2487.

Uduji, J.I., Okolo-Obasi, N.V.E., Nnabuko, J.O., Ugwuonah, G.E. and Onwumere, J.U. (2024), "Mainstreaming gender sensitivity in cash crop market supply chains: the role of CSR in Nigeria's oil producing communities", Journal of Agribusiness in Developing and Emerging Economies, Vol. ahead-of-print No. ahead-of-print.

Wake, N.J. (2015), "The use of the balanced scorecard to measure knowledge work", International Journal of Productivity and Performance Management, Vol. 64 No. 4, pp. 590-602.

Wills, G., Kennedy, S.H., Cheese, J. and Rushton, A. (1990), "Maximizing Marketing Effectiveness", Management Decision, Vol. 28 No. 2.

Wong, J., Ortmann, A., Motta, A. and Zhang, L. (2016), "Understanding Social Impact Bonds and Their Alternatives: An Experimental Investigation", Experiments in Organizational Economics (Research in Experimental Economics, Vol. 19), Emerald Group Publishing Limited, Leeds, pp. 39-83.

Yang, Y., Li, X., Zeng, D. and Jansen, B.J. (2018), "Aggregate effects of advertising decisions: A complex systems look at search engine advertising via an experimental study", Internet Research, Vol. 28 No. 4, pp. 1079-1102.

Zahoor, A. and Sahaf, M.A. (2018), "Investigating causal linkages in the balanced scorecard: an Indian perspective", International Journal of Bank Marketing, Vol. 36 No. 1, pp. 184-207.

Zameer, H., Wang, Y. and Yasmeen, H. (2024), "Strengthening green competitive advantage through organizational learning and green marketing capabilities in a big data environment: a moderated-mediation model", Business Process Management Journal, Vol. ahead-of-print No. ahead-of-print.

Zekos, G.I. (2003), "MNEs, globalization and digital economy: legal and economic aspects", Managerial Law, Vol. 45 No. 1/2, pp. 1-296.

Zhan, W., Jiang, M. and Li, C. (2021), "The service strategy of customer-intensive services under advertising effects", Kybernetes, Vol. 50 No. 8, pp. 2453-2470.

Zimand-Sheiner, D. and Earon, A. (2019), "Disruptions of account planning in the digital age", Marketing Intelligence & Planning, Vol. 37 No. 2, pp. 126-139.

Zineldin, M. and Philipson, S. (2007), "Kotler and Borden are not dead: myth of relationship marketing and truth of the 4Ps", Journal of Consumer Marketing, Vol. 24 No. 4, pp. 229-241.

www.ingramcontent.com/pod-product-compliance
Lightning Source LLC
Chambersburg PA
CBHW070410230526
45471CB00006B/2731